FIREMAN SAM'S 1 2 3

Illustrated by The County Studio

HEINEMANN • LONDON

1 one

Fireman Sam is showing Sarah and James
round the fire station. "We have one fire engine,"
he says, when they arrive.
"She's called Jupiter!" cries Sarah.

2   two

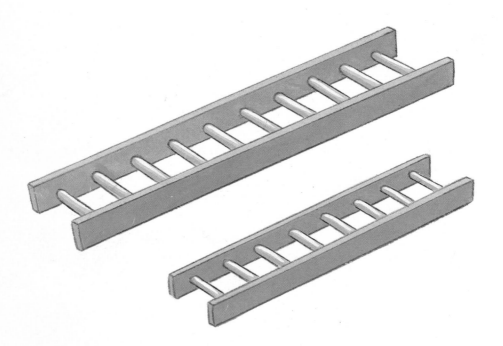

"We use ladders when we rescue people
from tall buildings," explains Fireman Sam.
"The two ladders are on top of Jupiter."

3   three

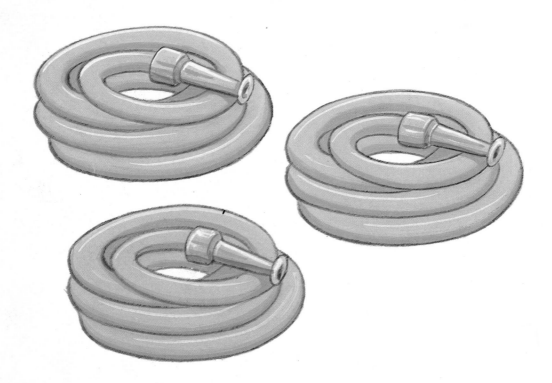

"The three hoses spray strong jets of water onto the flames to put out a fire quickly," continues Fireman Sam.

4   four

"What are those?" asks Sarah.
"Those are fire extinguishers," says Fireman Sam.
"We use them for putting out different types of fires."

5 five

Then Fireman Sam goes into the equipment room.
"Why are there five helmets, Uncle Sam?" asks James.
"There's one for Station Officer Steele, one for Elvis,
Trevor and me, and a spare one!"

James and Sarah help Fireman Sam wash Jupiter. While they are busy, Elvis arrives for work.

How many sponges can you see?
Can you find three birds?
How many wheels has Jupiter got?

6   six

When they finish washing Jupiter, they put the buckets
away in the garage. There are six buckets altogether.

7   seven

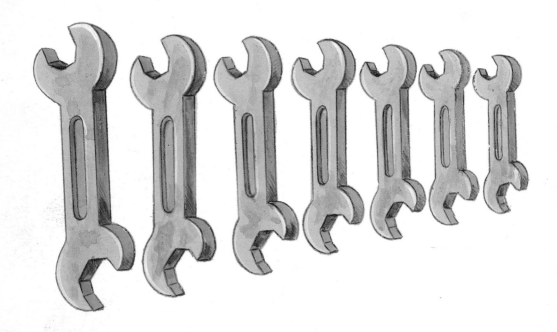

"What are those for, Uncle Sam?" asks Sarah.
"Elvis and I use those seven spanners to keep Jupiter in good condition."

8   eight

Next, they go inside the fire station. Elvis shows
them his food cupboard.
"*Eight* tins of beans, Elvis!" laughs James.
"Well, Sam says I can't cook anything else!"
replies Elvis.

9 nine

Trevor comes to the fire station to see everyone.
"I've got a present for us from Bella," he says,
holding up a box. The box has nine cakes in it!

10   ten

Before they have tea, James and Sarah help
Fireman Sam check the equipment.
"This pair of boots is getting old," says Fireman Sam.
"We must get some more."

Elvis makes some tea and they enjoy
Bella's cakes together.

How many chairs can you see?
Can you find three saucepans?
How many plates can you see?

Later, Fireman Sam and Elvis show James and Sarah
how quickly they can prepare for an emergency.
"You're a hero, Uncle Sam!" cries James.
"So are you, Elvis!" yells Sarah.

William Heinemann Ltd, Michelin House,
81 Fulham Road, London SW3 6RB

LONDON MELBOURNE AUCKLAND

First published 1992 by William Heinemann Ltd
Fireman Sam copyright © 1985 Prism Art & Design Ltd
Text copyright © 1992 William Heinemann Ltd
Illustrations copyright © 1992 William Heinemann Ltd
Based on the animation series produced by
Bumper Films for S4C – Channel 4 Wales –
and Prism Art & Design Ltd
Original idea by Dave Gingell and Dave Jones,
assisted by Mike Young
Characters created by Rob Lee

ISBN 434 96099 3

Produced by Mandarin Offset
Printed and bound in Hong Kong